Original title:
Dandelions in the Wind

Author: Arabella Whitmore
ISBN HARDBACK: 978-1-80566-598-4
ISBN PAPERBACK: 978-1-80566-883-1

Unraveled Secrets of Spring

Little wishes take to flight,
Chasing daylight, what a sight!
They dance and twirl, so carefree,
Tickling noses, look at me!

Freckles of laughter in the air,
Bouncing dreams without a care.
Whispers of mischief on the breeze,
Sowing giggles among the trees.

Puffs of Lightness

Fluffy clouds of yellow cheer,
Floating off without a fear.
They pop and giggle, scatter fast,
As nature's jesters, they amass.

A playful push, a gentle toss,
Each one lives, none is lost.
Rolling laughs on breezy trails,
Tickling toes and lightening gales.

Timeless Travels of Fluff

Puffy travelers ride the gust,
With tiny giggles, float we must!
Adventures born in a single puff,
Every journey's filled with stuff.

We swerve and swirl, a funny race,
Chasing shadows in a green space.
No map in hand, just whimsy bright,
Through fields of laughter, pure delight.

The Elegy of the Air

Oh, dear fluff, so light and spry,
With each soft tug, you kiss the sky.
A chuckle here, a snicker there,
In the lightheartedness we share.

You play with fate on zephyr's tease,
Tickling fancies with playful ease.
In every fall, a giggle sings,
The gentle joy that springtime brings.

Nature's Soft Confetti

Tiny seeds take to the skies,
Leaving trails of yellow surprise.
With each gust, they whirl and twirl,
Nature’s party, giving a twirl.

They land on noses, just for fun,
Tickling kids who laugh and run.
In fields they dance with gleeful cheer,
Who knew plants could bring such jeer?

Carried by Invisible Currents

A toss of fluff, oh so sly,
Up they go, like popcorn in the sky.
Sprightly whispers on the breeze,
They slip away with laughable ease.

Round and round they spin and race,
A game of tag in open space.
Chasing dreams, they hide and seek,
A wild show from nature's cheek.

Ephemeral Wishes in Flight

With every puff, a wish takes wing,
As they soar, giggles cling.
A friend shouts loud, 'Catch them, oh!
But they disappear—just like snow!'

They dance like jesters, light and free,
Transforming fields into a spree.
Fleeting hopes cascade from above,
A funny flutter filled with love.

Golden Dreams on a Gale

Golden fluff on the wind's embrace,
Whirling dreams without a trace.
They twinkle in the sun's warm glow,
Making wishes, putting on a show.

“Catch me!” cries the cheeky seed,
But they’re too fast, they’ll never heed.
With every gust, more giggles rise,
A dance of whimsy in blue skies.

Echoes of the Unseen Path

Tiny seeds take flight, oh what a sight,
They dance and twirl, with pure delight.
A gust of wind, a little shove,
They swirl around like they're in love.

Watch them tumble, bouncing in glee,
Wiggling about, they're wild and free.
A race with the breeze, they surely win,
Chasing after dreams on a whim.

Golden Wishes in a Tuscan Sky

Up in the air, they wave goodbye,
With whispers of wishes, they float and fly.
Golden dreams scattered, what a spread,
Each little fluff has something to shed.

With sunlit laughter, they shimmy and shake,
Turning the path into a wild cake.
Sprinkling giggles with every swirl,
Who knew nature had so much to unfurl?

The Ephemeral Dance of Nature’s Breath

A frolicsome drift, what a crazy race,
They tumble and giggle, no time to waste.
On a merry spree, watch them all dart,
Each little puff has a playful heart.

With the giggles of grass and a twist of fate,
They scurry along, isn’t this great?
Floating on chuckles, no cares in sight,
The joy of their journey, pure and light.

Soft Murmurs of Transience

Little fluff balls with a penchant for fun,
Bouncing and bobbing, they're on the run.
In the gentle air, they take their cue,
Making merry mischief, just for you.

Twirling around like a circus show,
Who knew they had such a sprightly glow?
With giggles of nature, they float and sway,
Bringing laughter to the brightening day.

Seeds of Solitude Adrift

Tiny fluff on breezy flight,
Dancing through the day and night.
Whispers giggle in the air,
As I chase them without a care.

They dodge the dog, they fool the cat,
Wiggly bits in a game of pat.
Laughing at their crazy spins,
These little jokers know how to win.

Lullabies on a Gentle Gale

Blowing soft like playful dreams,
They tickle noses, stir up schemes.
A breeze that sings a silly tune,
As seeds drift off to meet the moon.

Caught in hair, they love a tease,
Floating round like giggling bees.
They twirl and whirl in joyful fray,
Turning ordinary into play.

A Symphony of Wandering Wishes

In a concert of yellow beams,
Float away on whimsy's dreams.
Each little seed a wish on high,
Sailing past with a winked eye.

With pops and pings they fly around,
Making mischief on the ground.
A marching band in every puff,
Saying, 'Life is silly enough!'

The Fragile Journey of Sunlit Souls

They flutter forth with cheeky grace,
Mischief made in a sunny place.
A playful race through fields of green,
Chasing giggles, they're rarely seen.

Each sprightly twist, a trickster's thrill,
As they tumble over every hill.
Through hand and heart, they skip and slide,
Whispering secrets, full of pride.

Whispers of a Wayward Seed

A fluff ball drifts, oh so spry,
It dances 'round, making friends on high.
With giggles mixed in the playful air,
It tickles the nose of the curious bear.

The breeze is a prankster, sly and spry,
As seeds zoom past like they're saying hi.
They race with the squirrels, a madcap spree,
Creating chaos while sipping tea.

Flight of the Golden Fluff

A puff of gold leaps, taking flight,
It swirls and whirls in sheer delight.
With each little gust, it leaps like a fool,
Chasing a butterfly, breaking every rule.

The sun is laughing, the trees do sway,
As fluff balls bounce like they're here to play.
A tumble here, a flip over there,
A slapstick performance beyond compare.

Dusk's Gentle Wanderers

As twilight settles, with shadows deep,
Little fluffy seeds start to leap.
They tickle the toes of the sleeping cat,
Who yawns and shakes off her fluffy hat.

Countless figures, each in a race,
Chasing the moon with a silly face.
In the fading light, they twirl and glide,
A comedy show in the evening tide.

Unruly Dreams on the Breeze

Here comes a puff, looking quite grand,
With dreams of adventures, oh so unplanned.
It flips through the fields, spilling with cheer,
Waving to daisies, saying, "I'm here!"

From one wacky prank to another it flows,
Drawing laughter from folks as it goes.
With giggles and wiggles, it makes its stand,
The mischief-maker of the land.

Whispering Wonders

Tiny seeds take flight, oh what a show,
They leap and spin, with no care to tow.
Chasing each other in a playful game,
The skies get giggly, their laughter the same.

Bright little parachutes dance in the breeze,
They twirl and they swirl, with such perfect ease.
Who knew such fluff could bring so much cheer?
Left to their fancies, they disappear near.

The Lightness of Being

A gust of wind, and off they go,
Tiny travelers, on a whim, they flow.
With no set destination, they float and sway,
Making clouds of fluff on a sunny day.

They dodge and they weave, the world their stage,
Every twist and turn, a new funny page.
Like little comedians, spreading their cheer,
With each little puff, they conquer the sphere.

Flight Paths of Nature’s Children

Look at them scatter, on a playful spree,
Each tiny wisp, so carefree and free.
A fluttering joke on a warm summer's morn,
The followers giggle, as new paths are born.

They ride on the breeze, with style so absurd,
Crashing in gardens, they’re quite the herd.
With mischievous grins, in a whimsical dance,
Nature’s little jesters, given a chance.

Nostalgic Flurries

Oh how we laughed as we chased them 'round,
Those fluffy little fellows that spun from the ground.
Each gust of laughter sent them aloft,
Memories of childhood, so pure and soft.

A race to the sky, we'd leap and we'd shout,
Watching them soar, never knowing doubt.
With every farewell, they twinkled and danced,
Leaving behind magic, as if by chance.

Light-Kissed Wanderers

Tiny seeds on breezy flights,
Dancing high, in carefree heights.
With a twirl, they spark delight,
Wandering free from morning's light.

In the park, they play hide and seek,
Stumbling on laughter, cheek to cheek.
They swirl around like silly kids,
Painting the sky as nature bids.

Puffing clouds in the sunny air,
Silly travelers without a care.
They tickle noses, tease the trees,
With their antics as light as breeze.

Every laugh, a petal's cheer,
Whispering dreams in summer's ear.
They float and giggle, oh so spry,
These light-kissed wanderers fly high!

Tethered to the Air

Fleeting wishes on a breeze,
Tethered lightly, a tease to please.
With every gust, they leap and twirl,
Spreading joy in a whirlwind whirl.

They pop and giggle, they bounce and play,
Tagging along with the wind's ballet.
Hitching rides on the carefree gusts,
Singing a tune that never rusts.

Catching laughter that drifts so light,
They whirl around in pure delight.
Hopping through the fields, knee-high,
Chasing each other, oh my, oh my!

Adventurers in the afternoon sun,
Bound to laughter, it’s all in fun.
They tickle the clouds, entertain the air,
Tethered to joy, they roam everywhere!

Moonlit Tales of the Meadow

In the hush of night, they prance,
Whispering secrets in a wild dance.
They twinkle bright under silver beams,
Creating mischief, living dreams.

With a flicker, they start a race,
Floating freely in their silk lace.
They giggle at owls who hoot and swoon,
Waltzing beneath the sleepy moon.

Every puff tells a funny tale,
Of clumsy leaps that never fail.
Chasing shadows, just for kicks,
They trip on starlight, what a mix!

In this meadow, laughter grows,
As the night wind in sweet circles flows.
Moonlit jesters, bold and spry,
Bouncing around as time slips by!

The Soft Resonance of Departure

Softly waving, a gentle goodbye,
With a giggle, they flirt and fly.
Carried off in a playful breeze,
Whispering tales of mishaps with ease.

Puffing up against the setting sun,
Every little seed, a joke begun.
They tease the flowers in their sway,
Stirring laughter, come what may.

As the sun dips, the fun ignites,
Daring the dusk to join their flights.
Floating off, they spark the night,
In a soft chorus of pure delight.

Departing lightly, they leave their mark,
In hearts aflutter, igniting a spark.
These tiny jesters, light and free,
Echo laughter in their playful spree!

Flight of the Fragile

Fluffy heads take to the sky,
Like tiny planes that float on by.
They twist and twirl with comical grace,
Chasing each other in a wild race.

Whispers giggle as they embark,
In the bright sun, they leave their mark.
A sneaky breeze plays hide and seek,
While puffy seeds begin to peek.

They dance on air, as if in jest,
Nature's own version of a game of chess.
With every puff, they laugh and spin,
Tiny travelers with a cheeky grin.

So off they go, with a wink and smile,
Floating away, mile by mile.
Creating chaos without a care,
In a whimsical jaunt through the summer air.

A Tapestry of Floating Whispers

Threads of white in a playful spree,
Twisting and turning, oh look at me!
They drift along, a joyful parade,
A soft explosion, no need to be afraid.

Bubbles of laughter as they soar high,
Mischievous sprites saying goodbye.
Caught in giggles, they sway and spin,
A colorful quilt of chuckles within.

They tickle the flowers, tease the trees,
Dancing merrily with the summer breeze.
Each little puff a tale to tell,
Of joyous journeys where they dwell.

With every gust, they flip and plop,
In a skyward jig, they never stop.
Creating a mess with a laugh so bright,
Little fluff balls bring pure delight.

Secrets of the Breezy Field

In the breeze, they sneak about,
Whispering tales with a childish shout.
Clusters giggle, a soft confab,
Plotting journeys in their fluffy cab.

Spritz of humor fills the air,
As they drift in a stylish flare.
They mingle with bees, causing a stir,
A fluffy frolic, that's for sure!

With every puff, the mischief grows,
As the dance of fluffiness proudly shows.
They tease the grass and tease the sun,
A silly squad that's always on the run.

In a game of chase through fields so wide,
They spin and twirl, with laughter as their guide.
In this whimsical quest, joy takes the lead,
Where tiny dreams of fluff set the speed.

Ethereal Journeys of Tiny Dreams

Tiny seeds with dreams to share,
Riding high in the open air.
They frolic lightly, like feathered friends,
Following whims as each journey wends.

With giggles that echo across the field,
They chase the clouds, adventures revealed.
Wobbly flights with a belly full of glee,
Each little globule sings, "Come follow me!"

Through fields of gold, they take their flight,
In a crazy ballet, they spark delight.
As soft as a sneeze, and quick as a blink,
They dance in the day, while the world stops to think.

At twilight's call, they find a new home,
A cozy nook where they dream and roam.
In the moonlight's glow, they chuckle anew,
Tiny dreams take flight, as all dreams do.

Soft Souls on the Wind

Whispers frolic in the air,
Tiny travelers without a care.
They tickle noses, tease the trees,
And dance like laughter on the breeze.

Floating fluff in a playful race,
Each little puff finds its own space.
A wobbly waltz, a jig so spry,
Who knew such fun could fly so high?

They gather round with a giggle or two,
And tumble down like some silly crew.
Chasing shadows, seeking the sun,
Life's a party, and they've just begun!

So next time you see soft bits spread wide,
Think of the joy that they seem to ride.
A small reminder, oh what a sight,
That fun is endless, taking flight!

Ephemeral Passages of Nature

In nature's jest, she blows a kiss,
Little fluffs twirl, can't resist.
With every gust, they shimmy and sway,
Taking mischief on a sunny day.

They scatter seeds with joyful glee,
Sprouting laughter, can't you see?
Whirling spins, they twine and twist,
A comedy act not to be missed!

Across the fields, on a breezy quest,
Soft souls of joy know how to jest.
Landing lightly, a giggle shared,
In nature’s ballet, they’re never scared.

With each small hop, they find their way,
To sprinkle smiles, come what may.
In the grand ballet of life, they gleam,
A frolicking joke, a whimsical dream!

The Breath of Sprouted Freedom

Oh, frothy fluff, what a silly sight,
You bounce and swirl, pure delight.
A hiccup of laughter blows you soon,
A tiny balloon, a cheeky boon!

Like giggling whispers that float so high,
You've mastered the art of aiming for the sky.
Sprinkling cheer on the ground below,
In your breezy pirouette, you steal the show!

With a puff and a bounce, you roll away,
The world your dance floor, come what may.
Performing pirouettes like stars of a play,
What tiny jesters in the light of the day!

From polka dots to soft white fluff,
Your travels spark with giggles, enough!
In every nook, you leave a trace,
A reminder that life's a funny race!

A Dance with the Breath of Life

Gentle whispers tease the air,
As sprightly puffs prance without a care.
With a hop and a skip, they start to spin,
Their joyful frolics make the day begin!

Blowing kisses, they float so free,
Each little fluff is a sight to see.
With every giggle and playful blow,
They spread their joy, putting on a show!

In the dance of life, they twirl and glide,
With the sun as witness, they do not hide.
Sprouting laughter in the soft warm glow,
Leaving trails of cheer wherever they go.

So next time you spy a floating ball,
Remember it's just nature's call.
To laugh and dance, to swirl and spin,
A chuckle from nature—that's where we begin!

The Playground of the Air

A puff of fluff escapes the ground,
It dances high, it twirls around.
Little seeds with dreams to fly,
They tickle noses as they sigh.

Children laugh and chase with glee,
As tiny dreams adopt a spree.
They tumble down, a playful show,
Like silly whispers, to and fro.

Who knew a breath could spark such joy?
Like confetti tossed for every boy.
Nature’s jest in the sunny hour,
Sprouting giggles, seeds of power.

When one drifts past you in the breeze,
Pretend it’s telling jokes with ease.
Just don’t forget to make a wish,
Or let it go, like a goofy fish.

Weaving with the Wind

Catch the breeze, it's quite a game,
Tiny fluff is never tame.
It zigzags through the summer air,
Like a feathered daredevil fair.

Each little puff a mischief-maker,
A marionette for the sky's taker.
They plot their schemes in ranks so neat,
A parade of fun, oh what a treat!

I watched one cling to a curious bee,
It said, 'Come dance and fly with me!'
They spun and twirled, a waltz divine,
As blooms below began to shine.

So next time you see a twist and whirl,
Remember, life's a funny swirl.
Join the party, don’t just stand by,
And let your laughter touch the sky.

Celestial Seeds of Change

In galaxies of grassy dreams,
Seeds take flight, or so it seems.
A flip, a flurry, they scatter wide,
Becoming stars in the earth's great stride.

One twirled around a bumblebee,
It whispered, 'Follow! Come with me!'
They zoomed past kids in wild delight,
Creating chaos, a comical sight.

Life's a dash, a frolicsome race,
Each seed a grin, no time to brace.
As sunshine grins and giggles spread,
Seeds of laughter dance overhead.

So, let them soar wherever they please,
Watch as nature serves up these tease.
Shake a hand and feel the breeze,
As joy takes root with perfect ease.

Stories Written in the Sky

Fluffy seeds that dance and play,
A rogue breeze leads them astray.
Puffing cheeks, I blow a kiss,
They whirl and twirl, oh what bliss!

Up they go, a scattered plight,
Like tiny ships in morning light.
Each one tells a tale, you see,
Of all the fun they had with me!

Some get caught in a tree's embrace,
While others race in a silly chase.
They write their stories, oh so bold,
With laughter ringing, never old!

Watch them dance, a comical spree,
Sprinkled dreams, wild and free.
A sky full of chuckles, just take a peek,
Where giggles echo, all week!

Embracing the Tempest of Tomorrow

Blustery winds, what a surprise,
Whisking off furry little guys.
I chase them down with noodles long,
Who knew legumes could sing a song?

A gust, a swirl, they twirl around,
Landing softly without a sound.
I grab my hat, it takes to flight,
A wacky dance in the soft twilight!

Chasing fluff down the avenue,
They giggle back—what fun to pursue!
With every gust, a nutty dash,
As clouds above begin to clash!

Tomorrow's tempest, wild and bright,
A raucous party in sheer delight.
With tea and crumpets set to blow,
Who needs a plan when seeds can go?

Radiant Remnants of Yesterday

A fuzzy flurry from days gone by,
Like popcorn kernels in the sky.
In shock I pause, then start to grin,
These little puffs, where have you been?

Old tales wrapped in sunshine's glow,
Floating free, putting on a show.
Remember that time you gave me a fright?
Sailing past on a grand old kite!

With every puff, a chuckle swells,
In every swirl, a million spells.
Each story tickles my funny bone,
As past and present dance alone!

Radiance shining in every seed,
With giggles, they fulfill my need.
Who knew that laughter could float so high?
In remnants of joy, we'll touch the sky!

Sun-Kissed Farewells on the Horizon

Sunshine beams, as the fluffy fleet,
Goes tumbling on in a funny retreat.
Silly hats fly off in glee,
While I chase giggles, wild and free!

They jive and juke, a whimsical quest,
On the horizon, they dance with zest.
Like tiny balloons escaping from me,
What a sight, a childlike spree!

With every bounce, they wave goodbye,
As if they're saying, 'Don't you cry!'
I wave back, a silly grin,
And vouch to join the fun again!

So here's to the mirth, the skies ablaze,
Every farewell wrapped in rays.
A playful journey through laughs and light,
With a sun-kissed end, it feels just right!

Lost in Nature's Bounty

In a field of fluff, I trip and fall,
Wondering if I’m a part of it all.
The seeds escape like tiny balloons,
I chase them down, singing old tunes.

A dog runs past, with a glint in his eye,
He snatches a puff, and off he’ll fly.
I wave goodbye to my wispy friends,
Still hoping for joy that never ends.

Sunshine giggles, wind gives a sigh,
I laugh at the chaos; oh, my, oh my!
Petals swirl like a carnival ride,
I'm dizzy from nature's unplanned slide.

So here’s to mess, soon we’ll make noise,
A party of seeds, oh what are the joys!
In this wild world, I'll dance without care,
As floats my wish in the warm spring air.

The Magic of Transience

Whispers floating, a whimsical jest,
Life feels like a lively chest.
I try to catch them; they slip away,
Elusive dreams on a bright ballet.

One little puff said, "I'm the king!"
With a twist and a spin, he takes off to sing.
I laugh as I watch, oh what a scene,
Nature's confetti in a world so green.

A gust suddenly bursts my playful bubble,
Sending seeds flying, oh what a trouble!
I yell, "Hey, wait!" to the clouds above,
While chasing these moments I'm eager to love.

But in the end, they whirl and twirl,
Like mischievous kids in a cartwheel swirl.
So I'll gather joy in each fleeting hour,
And dance with the breeze, oh, what power!

Seeding the Sky

Up in the air, does a seed throw a wish?
A dream like a kite, swaying, oh so swish.
I ponder as bits float from here to there,
If wishes come true, do I have to share?

With a wink from the sun, the sky feels alive,
Each little flake seems set to thrive.
My neighbor's cat leaps, with grand pursuits,
Chasing the puffs, in floral pursuits.

"Catch me if you can!" shouts the fluff with glee,
As the mischievous wind plays tricks on me.
We giggle together, this wild spring play,
Creating confetti in our own silly way.

But soon they're gone, like jokes that you tell,
Yet in this dance, I've discovered a spell.
So next time I stumble, tripping in cheer,
I'll follow the seeds with nothing to fear.

Fragile Journeys of Hope

Off they go, on a gusty quest,
Tiny travelers, they seem so blessed.
Each fluffy head has a dream to chase,
As they bounce to the rhythm, a lively race.

I watch in awe, giggling away,
As fluffy ideas drift, sway, and play.
A wobbly breeze tickles my cheek,
Oh, what a joy! A laugh I seek.

Silly wishes on footloose wings,
Playful whispers of all the things.
Each little fluff knows just what to do,
From ground to the sky, they start anew.

So here's to the wisps, both bold and meek,
Carrying laughter, a world so unique.
In this fragile journey, hope takes a turn,
As we dance through the fluff, and our hearts learn.

Serenade of Wandering Seeds

A tiny parachute takes flight,
With dreams of landing in the light.
They giggle past a bumblebee,
As if they're daring it to flee.

Chasing blades of grass, they race,
Each little fluff a playful face.
They swirl around the laughing child,
In breezy chaos, sweet and wild.

An acorn calls, 'Let's start a game!',
While sunbeams cheer, they stake their claim.
Like jumpy clowns on summer's stage,
They twirl away, the meadow's page.

With every gust, they squeal and soar,
Who knew a breeze could ask for more?
In a giggly dance, they make their bid,
To be the stars, but never hid.

Hushed Stories of the Meadow

In silence, whispers fill the day,
As seeds prepare to drift and play.
'Oh! Look at us!' they all exclaim,
'Who knew a breeze could make us famous!'

With careful spins, they twirl about,
Dodging ants and clouds, no doubt.
They plot a path to who-knows-where,
Perhaps to join a bard's wild hair?

Each one a tale, spun from the fluff,
Of journeys bright, of fluffiness enough.
Laughing at the squirrels' parade,
They coast on dreams, no debts to trade.

Among the flowers, they hold a chat,
As petals chuckle at a splat.
With every gust, there's quite a stir,
More fun than being stuck in fur!

Moments Caught in a Zephyr

A gust of luck, a twist of fate,
Whispers secrets, oh so great.
They mingle with the summer's glee,
As butterflies all dance for free.

With every puff, new pals they meet,
A frolicsome game, oh so sweet.
Around the roses, laughter bounces,
While bees with jangling joy still trounces.

Each fluffy hope is on a quest,
To find a spot where they can rest.
They zigzag, tumble, pirouette,
Outwitting squirrels, never a fret!

Count the clouds, they're on a spree,
Floating wishes, come dance with me!
In shorts and shades, they take the lead,
Moments to share, in laughter's seed.

Detached from the Root

Free from the earth, they take a leap,
With giggles soft and feelings deep.
Floating high, they twist and twirl,
Bright tiny nomads in a whirl.

They wave goodbye to roots below,
And picnic with the winds that blow.
These tiny jesters, hearts so wide,
On laughter's breeze, they dance with pride.

With every shift, their tales unfold,
Of hopping hedgehogs, and joys of old.
No care for mud or rainy days,
Just hop along in bright sun's rays!

They sing of joy and grassy beds,
Of spider webs and lanky threads.
Through every gust, they find delight,
Turning the mundane to magic's flight!

Wishful Thoughts in the Air

Fluffy seeds dance with glee,
Chasing clouds, wild and free.
Each puff a wish, light and spry,
Floating up to the sky.

They dodge the trees with a laugh,
Taking the playful path.
What's this? A cat, a dog?
All joining in the fog!

Who knew dreams could take flight,
In the morning's soft light?
With giggles, they twist and twirl,
A whimsical, fluffy swirl.

So let's join this grand parade,
Where worries simply fade.
With each tickle of the breeze,
We'll dance among the leaves.

Harvested Dreams of the Breeze

Laughter sprouts with every blow,
Puffs of wishes start to flow.
Gypsy dreams in a breezy swirl,
Adventures waiting, give it a whirl.

Oh look! A giggle takes flight,
Tickling noses, oh what a sight!
Catching laughs in tiny jars,
Counting blessings like shooting stars.

A butterfly joins the spree,
Sipping nectar, oh so free.
Every flutter brings a cheer,
Whirling fun draws us near.

Let’s ride this jovial tide,
On this giggling, fluffy ride.
With thankful hearts, we'll embrace,
The magic of this happy space.

A Symphony of Softness

Whispers float on the gentle air,
Softness sings without a care.
A choir of giggles, what a sound,
As fluffy dreams leap all around.

Twists and tumbles, what a sight,
Wishes swirl, taking flight.
Each fluffy note brings a cheer,
Fleeting moments, oh so dear.

They dance in pairs, giggling bright,
A comic show, pure delight.
Puffing magic without a sound,
Joyful antics all around.

So join the laughter, let’s not hide,
With smiles tucked in, we’ll glide.
In this soft and silly tune,
We’ll bounce our way to the moon.

Fragility in Motion

A tickle of whimsy fills the breeze,
Soft little spores float with ease.
In the air, they twist and play,
Like little jesters on display.

Watch them wobble, giggle, spin,
Each tiny puff carries a grin.
A parade of feathers, light as air,
Tickling trees without a care.

They dodge the sun with a funny dance,
Taking every silly chance.
A tumble, a bounce, they're off again,
In this game without an end.

Let's cherish this playful sight,
Where fragility takes flight.
With laughter wrapped around our hearts,
We'll savor joy as it departs.

Silken Dances of Innocence

Little puffs float high with glee,
They tickle the noses of the bee.
On a breeze, they take a spin,
Giggles ensue as the fun begins.

A child rushes, arms out wide,
Trying to catch what won't abide.
The fluffy balls just laugh and sway,
Oh, how they love this silly play!

With every pounce, they dodge and weave,
A jesting dance that none believe.
They pirouette, then tumble down,
The playful jesters of the town.

As shadows waltz upon the grass,
They spread their cheer, a joyous mass.
With each small puff, the world anew,
Who knew such fun from seeds could brew?

The Spirited Journey of Sprouts

Tiny soldiers in a bright parade,
Marching small, but never afraid.
With each gust, they sway and sway,
Declaring, 'Let's dance another day!'

They scatter forth, a wild brigade,
Chasing dreams in a leafy glade.
Caught in laughter, they tumble down,
The fanciest hats of the earth's crown.

A gust of wind, a playful shove,
They spread their joy, with a little shove.
And off they go, like kites in flight,
Adventuring till the fall of night.

On wandering paths, they twirl and glide,
Finding new homes, oh what a ride!
With every leap, they giggle aloud,
The sprightly troupe that's nature's crowd.

Beyond the Garden's Edge

Beyond the fence where laughter lies,
Whimsical seeds take to the skies.
They glide away on a sunny spree,
Oh, how they dance, wild and free!

With a puff and a twist, they start to roam,
Leaving behind their garden home.
No one can catch these flighty beings,
In fields of green, they share their gleanings.

They tickle the toes of passersby,
As they sway and bounce, oh my, oh my!
With a wink and a giggle, they spread their cheer,
Making the mundane feel like a frontier.

From town to town, they skip and hop,
On breezy notes, they never stop.
Each tiny puff a little jest,
Sending smiles on a merry quest.

Ghosts of Past Blooms

In the twilight, shadows loom,
Of laughter, seeds, and bright blooms' room.
Whispers of petals take to night,
As memories swirl, a fleeting flight.

They dance like ghosts in the fading sun,
Reminiscing the laughter of everyone.
With every swirl, a tale they tell,
Of sunny days and the laughs that fell.

Once they were flowers, now they're just dreams,
But oh, how they giggle, or so it seems!
Transcending time, their laughter fades,
Yet still, they dance in the twilight shades.

A flicker of joy in a dusky glow,
As they twirl, the memories flow.
With each small puff, a story dwells,
In every heart, their laughter swells.

Tales of the Airborne

Up they rise, with a puff of cheer,
Little balloons, no hint of fear.
Off they go, on a breezy spree,
Chasing clouds, just like me!

They tumble and dance, in a twisty flight,
Winky faces, oh what a sight!
A giggle here, a wiggle there,
Floating dreams in the bright blue air.

In the park, they claim their thrones,
Swirling whispers, and silly tones.
Kids and pups, all join the game,
Chasing buddies without a name.

So let them spin, like wild confetti,
Each one laughing, oh so free and jetty.
Tales of the airborne, so light and spry,
With giggles galore, they wave goodbye!

A Cascade of Gentle Whispers

Whispers gliding, soft as lace,
Ticklish secrets, a breezy race.
Hats off, don’t lose that crown!
Here comes the gust, swirl around!

Peek-a-boo, from tree to tree,
Fluffy giggles, come play with me!
Silly sprigs in a merry ride,
With frolicsome gales, no fear to hide.

As they tumble, they twirl and spin,
Caught in laughter, where jokes begin.
Twirling round with a cheeky spin,
Floating pleasures, let the fun begin!

So join the dance of this joyous fleet,
With every puff, life’s not discreet.
A cascade of whispers, floating light,
In this merry dance, all hearts take flight!

Fleeting Fancies of a Quiet Heart

Fleeting fancies, oh what delight,
Bouncing dreams take to the height.
A gentle nudge, a playful tease,
Whisked away, just like a breeze.

They scatter wide, like bursts of giggles,
Swaying softly, with little wiggles.
A moment's joy, then off they scoot,
To chase a rainbow, in funny pursuit.

Their laughter echoes, crisp and free,
In a subtle dance, oh so carefree.
What's the rush? Let moments spar,
With whispers sweet, just like a star.

In the quiet, see them parade,
Making mischief, in sunshine's shade.
Fleeting fancies take us away,
To funny places where hearts can play!

Embracing the Invisible

Embracing what we cannot see,
Giggling breezes, full of spree.
Invisible friends, oh how they play,
In each flutter, they steal away.

Nudged by the gust, they take a chance,
Doing the can-can in a dance.
With every gust, a chuckle flies,
A tickle bomb in the sunny skies.

They spin a tale, of unseen fun,
Bouncing high like a playful bun.
Captured moments, swift as light,
Invisible capers, pure delight!

So let us join this merry song,
Laughing together, where we belong.
Embracing the invisible is the key,
To find the joy in all we see!

Tumbleweeds of Radiance

A fluffball rolls by, oh how it darts,
A little yellow crown with brave, silly parts.
It giggles and tumbles, a dance on parade,
Chasing the sunshine, a jester in jade.

It bounces and bobs, with no thought of care,
Teasing the rocks, oh, what a wild air!
With whispers of chaos, it leads the grand chase,
In this goofy ballet, we all find our place.

Round and around, it’s a comedic delight,
A comedy act under the soft moonlight.
With every gust, we share in its fluff,
Puff, giggle, repeat; oh, this is enough!

So here’s to the folly, the whims and the cheer,
To the tipsy little bits that knock us off gear.
Let laughter abound in this whimsical wind,
For life’s too short not to dance on a whim.

The Dazzle of Distant Days

In fields of bright laughter, they spin and they sway,
Tiny suns shining, inviting us to play.
With each little gust, they whirl through the air,
Creating a chaos that's devil-may-care.

They whisper sweet secrets, a raucous delight,
Spinning around like balloons in the night.
In search of fine mischief, they dance with the breeze,
Unruly and merry, they tease as they tease.

Oh, what a spectacle, this jolly parade,
We join in the revel, no plans to evade.
With giggles and gambols, we follow the mad,
For chasing such joy makes the serious bad.

So tickle your senses, let folly abound,
In a dance with the haloes that tumble around.
For every small moment that brightens the day,
Is a treasure to savor, come join in the play!

Elysian Airborne Sorrows

On a gusty adventure, a lighthearted crew,
Fluff and whimsy are all we pursue.
They topple and twirl, with not a care in sight,
Creating a ruckus like purest delight.

With spins and cha-chas, they take to the skies,
Creating a rapture that tickles the eyes.
A paradox breezes, of laughter and air,
In this circus of fluff, we find none to spare.

They waltz with the zephyr, oh what merry jest!
Tickling the clouds, in a fluff-fueled quest.
With sorrow disarmed, we abandon the frown,
And join in the magic that wears a bright crown.

So giggle aloud as they sail and they swoosh,
Nothing's more joyful than a soft little push.
With colegas of sunshine, together we race,
For fun is the mission, in this bouncy embrace!

Serendipity's Breath

The breeze plays mischief with cheeky delight,
Carrying laughter through day and through night.
With each soft landing, it tumbles with glee,
A burst of pure joy, oh, what could it be?

A golden confetti, it leaps from the grass,
Out of the way, as we watch it all pass.
It tickles our noses, it dances our dreams,
In fits of giggles, or so it seems.

Oh, chase it and catch it, this whimsical sprite,
That fills up our hearts with a hug oh-so-tight.
Let silliness bloom as it frolics and flies,
May we all find the wonder in ever surprise.

So let your worries just flit and dissolve,
In the playful chaos that we all evolve.
With humor our compass and laughter our thread,
We whirl with the wonders, perfectly led!

Celestial Seeds of Fortuity

Tiny fluff on a flight,
Where the giggles take their height.
Sprouting dreams that waltz and twirl,
Playful whispers in a whirl.

Bouncing off a shoe or hat,
Dodging dogs, and oh! That cat.
Each puff holds a wish on deck,
As I dodge a curious peck.

Mementos in the Swirling Air

Tiny bits that chuckle loud,
In the breeze, they form a crowd.
They dance like stars in a giggle spree,
Unruly charm like chaos, free.

A child's laughter ignites the chase,
As tiny seeds swirl in wild grace.
With each puff, forget the woes,
In this game, hilarity grows.

The Art of Letting Go

Release a wish, just throw it out,
Watch it twist, tangle, and shout.
Hopes take off in bursts of fun,
A comedy show under the sun.

With every breeze, a giggly sigh,
As fortune taunts and flits on by.
Hold your heart and chase a whim,
In the mess, life's joys brim.

Whimsy Amongst the Charms of Night

Seeds perform their evening dance,
In moonlit air, they take their chance.
They tickle noses, weave their tales,
Like tiny boats with merry sails.

Giggles echo in the dark,
Each seed, a little sparkling spark.
In the night, they spin and play,
Whimsy paints the sky’s ballet.

Sunshine's Embrace on the Horizon

Little puffs on the green,
Chasing dreams, oh so keen.
Tickling noses, what a sight,
Spinning round in pure delight.

As they swirl and twirl about,
Who knew plants could jump and shout?
With a giggle, they take flight,
Bouncing off with all their might.

Sunshine winks at every turn,
What a dance, oh how they yearn.
In the field, a playful jest,
Nature’s laughter, at its best.

Tiny parachutes in air,
Fluffy travelers without a care.
Silly seeds, on breezes play,
Making merry on their way.

Chasing the Fleeting Flurry

Up in the air, a fuzzy foe,
With a laugh, they steal the show.
Popping up like happy springs,
Ready now for all the flings.

On a breeze they'll make a run,
Chasing tails, oh what fun!
Round and round, they laugh and weave,
Daring all to just believe.

A game of tag with little coax,
Fumbling friends, like merry folks.
Catching gold in every blow,
Spreading joy with every throw.

Oh the silly sights they make,
With every twist, and every shake.
A bubbly rush, not hard to see,
Life’s a frolic, wild and free.

Whispers of the Seed

Tiny fluff with stories to tell,
Whispering in the sunlight's swell.
Sassy seeds, oh so spry,
Giggle in the open sky.

They twirl like dancers with flair,
No worries, nothing to compare.
Ticklish breezes laugh anew,
Playing hide and seek, we pursue.

A gentle nudge, they take a spin,
Off they go, oh let the fun begin!
The world a stage, a grand parade,
With joy so sweet, they'll never fade.

Moments dance in the sky above,
Seeds of laughter and dreamy love.
In every gust, they skip and play,
Fun-filled stories lead the way.

Fleeting Hopes on a Breeze

Fluffy whispers on the run,
Giggling seeds beneath the sun.
Hopes and dreams all dressed in white,
Floating off with sheer delight.

Puffy clouds with playful glee,
Spreading joy, oh can't you see?
With every gust, they leap and prance,
Inviting all to join the dance.

Silly friends on a whimsy ride,
On the currents, they slip and slide.
Chasing giggles, they weave and bound,
In the air, laughter's the sound.

Each little puff a wish takes flight,
Spreading cheer, oh what a sight!
Fleeting moments, bright and bold,
In this game, let joy unfold.

Carried by Currents of Hope

Little seeds on an airy ride,
Tumbling through the sky so wide.
They dance and swirl with joyful glee,
As if each one has a whimsy key.

Floating high, then dipping low,
These tiny wonders steal the show.
With giggles from the gusty cheer,
They prank the flowers, year by year.

A fluffy fuzzball has a plan,
To reach the garden, it's the man.
But oops! It lands in a dog’s fur,
Now that’s a tale to stir and purr!

So let them twirl, let them sway,
To scatter dreams along the way.
In every puff, a laugh we find,
As whispered wishes, sweet and blind.

Ethereal Hues of the Unbound

Whispers of yellow in the air,
Inkling that something's everywhere.
Sprightly sprouts that tease the grass,
Dancing legs, oh what a class!

Each petal like a tiny kite,
Floating off in pure delight.
They can't decide which way to go,
A raucous plot, a cheeky show!

Some dreams are stuck in muddy shoes,
While others chase away the blues.
What's more amusing than a race,
Of fluff and flutters, out of place?

Chasing giggles, what a game!
They twist and turn, they're never tame.
A crafty breeze, what fun it lends,
To wandering whims, oh how it bends!

Fleeting Days in Echoed Breezes

Wandering whispers weave and wend,
Through fields where giggles never end.
In a sweep, they float and glide,
Chasing each other, side by side.

Chasing sunshine, they take flight,
Incredibly unbothered by height.
They twirl like confetti in a gale,
Each bounce a story, each drift a tale.

They play tag with a bumblebee,
"Oh no, don't catch me!" they tease with glee.
A merry flop on a sunlit patch,
Then off again, making a match.

In wobbly whirls, in flouncy shows,
These cheeky fluffballs strike their pose.
With every breeze, they lift the heart,
For fun, my friends, is a work of art!

Wild Wishes on Carefree Currents

Puffs of giggles take to flight,
Skyward bound in sheer delight.
Each fleeting wish is light as air,
A sprinkle of fun beyond compare.

Whirling, twirling in the sun,
What a crazy, silly run!
They dodge the raindrops, leap the creeks,
With every flutter, laughter speaks.

Look at them bounce on a breeze so keen,
Playing hide and seek with the green.
No one knows where they will land,
Each little fluff is a life unplanned.

Spinning tales with every gust,
Floofy future, a must!
So here’s the secret we can't defend:
Life’s a confetti, my fluffy friend!

The Journey of a Wish

Once a puffball danced with glee,
It twirled and swirled, so wild and free.
With every gust, it laughed aloud,
A tiny globe, so proud and bowed.

Off it flew, past bushes and trees,
Tickling squirrels, swaying with ease.
"Catch me if you can!" it did proclaim,
But the wind just laughed, playing the game.

It tumbled and spun through meadows bright,
Chasing butterflies, what a sight!
With a wink and a flip, it waved bye-bye,
Heading for dreams beneath the sky.

And though it vanished, clear as day,
The laughter lingered, in a playful way.
In every heart, a little wish grows,
Like a silly thought, no one really knows.

Nature's Wandering Souls

Tiny seeds in the air do play,
Whirling around, in a carefree way.
A gust of wind, oh what a ride!
Like tiny boats on a joyful tide.

One bumped a bee, who spilled its tea,
"Hey, watch it!" buzzed the bee with glee.
They laughed and danced, what a hilarious pair,
The bee in a frenzy, and the seed in the air!

Past the flowers, they rolled and spun,
Competing for laughs, both having fun.
The bee said, "Quick! Let’s race to the sun!"
But the seed just giggled, knowing it’s won.

At the end of the day, up high it flew,
Leaving behind a sky so blue.
With a wink at the flowers, it bade adieu,
A chuckle echoed, as nature’s crew.

A Cascade of Sunlit Fancies

In the meadow where laughter grows,
A parade of dreams, all in a pose.
Each little fluff with a giggle to share,
Spreading joy everywhere, without a care.

Blowing off worries, like fluff off a cake,
Do they know the mischief they make?
Floating to places both near and far,
While imagining lands where the jellybeans are.

They tickle the clouds, causing bursts of mirth,
As if to remind us, of our own worth.
Each trip a delight, on this bright sunny day,
Where imagination and whimsy happily play.

So here’s to the fancies that float in the air,
Bringing a smile, banishing despair.
Like a wild child, without a tether,
They bounce and tumble, together forever.

Floating Wishes

A wish took flight on a giggly breeze,
Bobbing along with such silly ease.
"Watch me!" it squeaked, as it cruised by,
Dodging a pigeon that squawked in reply.

Past the park swings where children play,
It wobbled and wiggled, come what may.
Entangled in chuckles from faces so bright,
Turning mundane moments into pure delight.

It rolled down hills, through laughter and cheer,
Whispering secrets when someone was near.
"I dare you to catch me," it gleefully said,
As it zipped through the grass, carefree and spread.

And when it was lost, floating too far,
It just laughed and twinkled, a shooting star.
In every giggle, a wish took flight,
Floating forever, in the heart's soft light.

Remnants of Youth

In fields where giggles gently roam,
An age-defying, feathery foam.
They dance on whispers, oh so spry,
Claiming each moment, waving goodbye.

With little puffs of yellow cheer,
They float like dreams, oh so sincere.
A foolish flight, no time to rest,
In a world where time loves to jest.

They bounce on breezes, acting sly,
Like tiny dreams that laugh and sigh.
Chasing mischief with a swirling twirl,
As if they've just outsmarted the world.

So here we stand, chuckles abound,
While nature laughs without a sound.
In joyful chaos, life is spun,
In trails of laughter, never done.

The Sound of Softly Drifting

A thousand wishes float away,
On gentle winds that twist and sway.
Tickled by the sun's warm kiss,
They whisper secrets of pure bliss.

They scatter stories, wild and free,
Like tiny ships on a giggling spree.
With every puff, they tease the air,
A game of hide and seek laid bare.

Like whispers shared between old friends,
Their laughter trails as joy transcends.
They swirl and dance with pompous flair,
Unruly jesters in the sweet spring air.

Each playful twist brings cheeky grins,
In a world where silliness always wins.
As we watch them flee, light on their feet,
Chasing the wind, oh what a treat!

Echoes of the Meadow

The meadow hums with a lively tune,
As it welcomes spring beneath the moon.
A chorus of laughter fills the air,
With echoes lost in the breezy fair.

Each fluff a promise, a prank in disguise,
They tumble and roll under vast blue skies.
With every breath, a chuckle's spun,
They seek the sun, oh what fun!

Like little clowns in a spirited parade,
They find the fun in a game well played.
With whimsical hops to the grass below,
They spread the joy wherever they go.

In this nostalgic, laughter-filled delight,
Nature's jesters dance out of sight.
So let them drift, let them roam wide,
For in their mischief, joy can't hide.

Sweet Surrender to the Breeze

In a gentle swirl, they take their flight,
Waving goodbye in the fading light.
They twirl and giggle, carefree spills,
Draped in laughter, over the hills.

With a puff and a spin, they launch and dive,
Each little seed, feeling alive.
With soft, mushy hugs from the sweet spring air,
They tease and tumble without a care.

In every gust, they frolic and play,
Taking their time on this grand ballet.
Floating away, so light and free,
In a jest of nature, you and me.

Each breath of wind, a silly chase,
Wishing to linger in this happy place.
With every puff, let laughter bloom,
As the world spins on in a playful room.

Caught in the Sunlit Whirl

Tiny seeds take flight, oh what a sight,
Dancing high, filled with delight.
Tickled by the breeze, spinning around,
Landing on noses, giggles abound.

Floating feathers in a sunny glow,
Chasing after shadows, to and fro.
Who knew a puff could cause such cheer?
A mischief-maker, never fear!

With every gust, they swirl and sway,
Creating laughter in their playful way.
Oh, the joy of a carefree chase,
Try to catch them; they vanish with grace.

Whirling happiness in a playful race,
Conspirators of joy in the open space.
While we chase the warmth of fun-filled hours,
These tiny jesters bring us flowers.

Torn from Home

A slight gust snatches a tiny sprout,
Unceremoniously tossing about.
Home is left behind, what a bold jump!
Off they drift, with a whimsical thump.

A tumble here, a spiral there,
Landing in gardens without a care.
Plotting their reign in new land's embrace,
Making new homes while wearing a face.

Oh, what an uproar in every new town,
Planting their cheer, never a frown!
The locals look puzzled, the scene so absurd,
As laughter erupts, not a single word.

From the fields to the city, they happily stray,
Wandering off, what a curious play!
For what is home when you’re full of spright?
A cosmic joke, soaring into the light.

Drifted Thoughts in the Air

Thoughts float freely, ticklish and spry,
Zipping through the blue, oh my, oh my!
What was that notion, lost in a swirl?
Catching the breeze is quite the whirl.

A giggle of ideas, who's in the lead?
A chase for wisdom is all that we need.
Ideas tumble like leaves in the fall,
Some graceful, some wobbly, oh how they sprawl!

From wacky dreams to whimsical schemes,
Scattering joy, like bursting seams.
Laughter takes flight on the gentle air,
Splattered with nonsense, here, there, everywhere!

So let your mind drift, unhinged and free,
Compose a concerto in pastel glee.
Embrace the silliness in every thought,
For laughter's a treasure, never bought.

Dreams of a Vanishing Moment

A puff from a pot, a moment so brief,
Sailing through spaces, too wild for belief.
They vanish too quickly, a fleeting delight,
Leaving behind whispers in soft flight.

With giggles and grins, they twirl away,
Sharing quick tales from their wild ballet.
But blink, and they're gone, a memory made,
Fleeting, elusive, like shadows that fade.

Oh, what a game, this chase of a dream,
Laughter erupts as they rapidly stream.
With every tickle of whimsy in play,
Memories linger but refuse to stay.

In the quiet aftermath of the grand show,
We're left in the wake of the dance's flow.
An echo of joy leads the way to the past,
Chasing the laughter, we've had such a blast!

Timely Dances of Fate

In fields of fluff we prance and play,
Chasing whispers that giggle away.
With every puff, a wish takes flight,
And I vow to dance with all my might.

Each comet of white, a secret revealed,
Starts off as a thought, but soon is concealed.
We leap like rabbits, with glee we collide,
Finding joy in the chaos, the tales that we bide.

But off to the skies, our secrets can soar,
Tickling the clouds, oh, who could want more?
Our giggling wishes, like balloons in a race,
Who knew fate was such a funny old face?

With each passing breeze, we wave and we cheer,
As fate spins around with a flick of its ear.
So come be a part of this whimsical scene,
As we dance with the fluff, oh, how sweet life can glean!

Where Dreams Take Flight

Amidst the sparks of a lazy day,
Fluffy delights begin to sway.
We leap to the rhythm of wishes unspoken,
With tickle fights that leave us all broken.

A wished-for adventure, oh where will we land?
Chasing those whispers, hand-in-hand.
Laughter erupts as we run through the fun,
Finding joy in the moments and everyone.

Blown by the breeze, like balloons in a jest,
We follow our fancies, that's truly the best.
With silly old dreams dancing on the grass,
We giggle and shout, let's see who will pass!

So when fancies fly, oh, you can't get enough,
A ticklish magic, the world's full of fluff.
Hold on to the laughter, don't let it take flight,
In a sparkling dreamland, our hearts feel so light.

The Path of Softness

Upon this silky, gentlest path,
We waddle like ducks, all in a bath.
Fluffy surprises peek out with a grin,
They poke at our toes, saying, "Come on in!"

Breezy and bold, we giggle away,
On this wooshy journey, come join the play!
With each bouncing step, we laugh 'till we cry,
At the unexpected spins that zap us nearby.

Like candies that twirl on a sunbeam's delight,
We dart through the grass, oh, what a sight!
Softness beneath us, an invitation to sway,
With dreams that are fluffy, let's dance through the day.

So grab onto magic, with giggles galore,
As we bounce toward the sun, who could ask for more?
Each step is a chuckle, a silly affair,
On this playful soft path, you'll find laughter everywhere!

Silvery Hopes on the Wind

As moonlight tickles the night's gentle face,
We chase shimmering hopes at a whimsical pace.
With sparkly dreams floating high in the air,
We tumble through giggles, not a single care.

The breeze carries secrets, oh what can they be?
A tickle from fate, laughing joyfully.
We swirl with the stars, on this magical ride,
Catching the glow, letting smiles be our guide.

When wishes get caught in the gleam of the night,
We spin like whirlwinds, what a joyful sight!
With hearts made of sparkles, we'll frolic and weave,
In realms of adventures where we both believe.

So let's ride the whispers, let's follow the cheer,
Creating a melody for all who are near.
For silvery hopes on the breeze are divine,
So toss all your worries, come dance in the shine!

www.ingramcontent.com/pod-product-compliance
Lightning Source LLC
Chambersburg PA
CBHW072146200426
43209CB00051B/757
9781805665984